# First Picture Dictionary
## Animals
### 第一本图画词典
### 动物

Pig
猪

Rabbit
兔子

Butterfly
蝴蝶

Fox
狐狸

Illustrated by Anna Ivanir

www.kidkiddos.com
Copyright ©2025 by KidKiddos Books Ltd.
support@kidkiddos.com

All rights reserved. No part of this book may be reproduced in any form or by any electronic or mechanical means, including information storage and retrieval systems, without written permission from the publisher, except in the case of a reviewer, who may quote brief passages embodied in critical articles or in a review.
First edition, 2025

**Library and Archives Canada Cataloguing in Publication**
First Picture Dictionary - Animals (English Simplified Chinese Bilingual edition)
ISBN: 978-1-83416-411-3 paperback
ISBN: 978-1-83416-412-0 hardcover
ISBN: 978-1-83416-410-6 eBook

# Wild Animals
# 野生动物

Lion
狮子

Tiger
老虎

Giraffe
长颈鹿

✦ *A giraffe is the tallest animal on land.*
✦ 长颈鹿是陆地上最高的动物。

Elephant
大象

Monkey
猴子

# Wild Animals
## 野生动物

Hippopotamus
河马

Panda
熊猫

Fox
狐狸

Rhino
犀牛

Deer
鹿

**Moose**
驼鹿

**Wolf**
狼

✦ *A moose is a great swimmer and can dive underwater to eat plants!*

✦ 驼鹿是优秀的游泳者,还能潜入水中吃植物!

**Squirrel**
松鼠

**Koala**
树袋熊

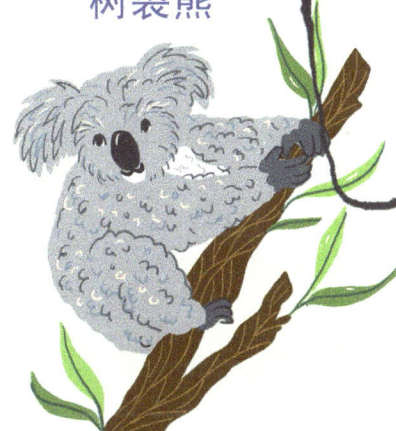

✦ *A squirrel hides nuts for winter, but sometimes forgets where it put them!*

✦ 松鼠会把坚果藏起来过冬,但有时会忘记藏在哪儿了!

**Gorilla**
大猩猩

# Pets
宠物

Canary
金丝雀

✦ *A frog can breathe through its skin as well as its lungs!*
✦ 青蛙不仅用肺呼吸，还能通过皮肤呼吸！

Guinea Pig
豚鼠

Frog
青蛙

Hamster
仓鼠

**Goldfish**
金鱼

**Dog**
狗

◆ *Some parrots can copy words and even laugh like a human!*

◆ 有些鹦鹉会模仿说话，甚至像人一样笑！

**Cat**
猫

**Parrot**
鹦鹉

Mosquito
蚊子

Dragonfly
蜻蜓

✦ *A dragonfly was one of the first insects on Earth, even before dinosaurs!*
✦ 蜻蜓是地球上最早出现的昆虫之一，比恐龙还早！

Butterfly
蝴蝶

Bee
蜜蜂

Ladybug
瓢虫

Badger
獾

Porcupine
豪猪

Groundhog
土拨鼠

◆ *A lizard can grow a new tail if it loses one!*
◆ 蜥蜴如果失去尾巴，可以长出新的！

Lizard
蜥蜴

Ant
蚂蚁

# Small Animals
# 小型动物

Chameleon
变色龙

Spider
蜘蛛

✦ *An ostrich is the biggest bird, but it cannot fly!*
✦ 鸵鸟是最大的鸟类，但它却不会飞！

Bee
蜜蜂

✦ *A snail carries its home on its back and moves very slowly.*
✦ 蜗牛把它的家驮在自己背上，移动的非常缓慢。

Snail
蜗牛

Mouse
老鼠

# Quiet Animals
## 安静的动物

Ladybug
瓢虫

Turtle
乌龟

✦ *A turtle can live both on land and in water.*

✦ 乌龟既能在陆地上生活，也能在水中生活。

Fish
鱼

Lizard
蜥蜴

Owl
猫头鹰

Bat
蝙蝠

✦ An owl hunts at night and uses its hearing to find food!

✦ 猫头鹰在夜间捕猎，用听觉来寻找食物！

✦ A firefly glows at night to find other fireflies.

✦ 萤火虫在夜间发光，是为了找到其他萤火虫。

Raccoon
浣熊

Tarantula
食鸟蛛

# Colorful Animals
## 色彩缤纷的动物们

A flamingo is pink
火烈鸟是粉红色的

An owl is brown
猫头鹰是棕色的

A swan is white
天鹅是白色的

An octopus is purple
章鱼是紫色的

A frog is green
青蛙是绿色的

✦ A frog is green, so it can hide among the leaves.

✦ 青蛙是绿色的，所以它可以藏在树叶中。

# Animals and Their Babies
动物和它们的宝宝

Cow and Calf
母牛和小牛

Cat and Kitten
猫和小猫

✦ *A chick talks to its mother even before it hatches.*
✦ 小鸡在孵化前就能和妈妈"说话"。

Chicken and Chick
母鸡和小鸡

Dog and Puppy
狗和小狗

**Butterfly and Caterpillar**
蝴蝶和毛毛虫

**Sheep and Lamb**
绵羊和小羊

**Horse and Foal**
马和小马

**Pig and Piglet**
猪和小猪

**Goat and Kid**
山羊和小羊

www.ingramcontent.com/pod-product-compliance
Lightning Source LLC
LaVergne TN
LVHW072055060526
838200LV00061B/4745